ENDING 60 YEARS
OF SOLITUDE

Ending 60 years of solitude – a portrait of a peace deal

Will Spurr

Contents

"for it's much cheaper down in the South American towns, where the miners work almost for nothing"

Bob Dylan, 'North Country Blues'

"el pueblo es superior de sus dirigentes. [The Pueblo is superior to its leaders]"

Jorge Eliecer Gaitán

Preface

Colombian history repeats itself; first as tragedy, then as FARC. Colombia's chronic coexistence with armed conflict has ebbed and flowed with painful cyclicality. A point not lost on Colombians; with the character Colonel Aureliano Buendia from Gabriel Garcia Marquez's *One Hundred Years of Solitude*, who not only lead the Liberal banner in count- less failed civil wars, but also lived to see iterative generations of his family take up his namesake, taking, I would argue, his name from the charac- ter Aurelian in Jorge Luis Borges' short story *The Theologians*, who spends out his days struggling to justify to himself the defence of linear time in favour of an ever repeating cycle, a debate that re- sulted in the violent death of his colleague.

The Colombian peace deal is no panacea, but if it is well implemented, it is a huge leap in the right direction. Consider this a bluffer's guide to the process that has scarcely touched Western minds beyond an occasional feature in the late night news; for it is neither an exhaustive academic investigation, nor does it offer any profound new insights. Rather, it is a portrait of a country in transition, a country that is redefining itself in contrast to a history of cyclical violence from which it wishes to escape.

In the construction of this short book, my gratitude is firstly owed to the Undergraduate Research Support Scheme, for funding my research on the peace deal – and the travels around the great nation the project entailed. On a similar note, I am thankful for the support and guidance of Professor Briony Jones, my research supervisor, for whom this small body of research may hopefully provide minor assistance in what I imagine will be a far more masterful forthcoming book on Transitional Justice. The various Colombian based academics, lawyers, NGO workers, and journalists who have given up their time to be interviewed by a disorientating undergraduate with a sub-par grasp of the Spanish language – despite the demands exacted upon by working in this nadir point of Colombian history. Of whom there are too many to spell out (and in some cases from a fear of putting them in any risk), however, special mention should go to the editor of the remarkable English language newspaper *Colombia Reports*, Adriaan Anselma, who remained insightful and engaging for the duration of a mammoth six-hour interview.

It would be unjust not to mention the cohort of friends and relations who have both helped this book come into existence, and tolerated my often frenetic ramblings regarding Colombian politics. Special thanks are due to my parents, for both stomaching and supporting my frequent and erratic decisions to enter questionably secure geopolitical regions, and to my long-suffering friend and co-editor in the Warwick-based satirical newspaper *The Hoar,* Will Kerry, who has kindly lent his skills as a freelance graphic designer to the end of making this book at the very least æsthetically pleasing.

In writing about a conflict that is intensely political – the intrusion of bias is inevitable. Where obvious, I have tried to curtail overt manifestations of said bias by providing an aggregate of available viewpoints, or by being uniformly critical of all parties involved. The only group in the conflict for whom I see little space for sympathies are the various paramilitary and paramilitary successor groups – including narco-traffickers and their private armies – who are a million miles away from simple self-defence groups, and have been a persistent thorn in the side of a meaningful peace, even to this day.

I have been lazy in referencing towards further banks of information, and hence should reiterate that this is not a rigorous academic work, but rather it is a collection of meandering reflections collected with the intention of providing an inaugural guide for those who understandably have neither the time nor volition to study the peace deal in considerable detail, yet wish to know more than just the bare bones of the process. For those wanting to engage in further reading, I have attached a bibliography of useful, though non-exhaustive, sources.

A country in transition

In Colombia, a loose historical cycle follows as such; wealth, land and power agglomerate in the hands of an elected oligarchy, unifying figures cry out for social justice, the movement organises, the powers that be quash the uprising by whatever force necessary, the rebellion returns to the drawing board, and so on. The actors change, but the result is always the same, violence. Countless arguments spell out that it is not a drive towards violence somehow innate in Colombians that causes the persistence of armed conflict, but the causes are instead egregious structural imbalances built upon fault lines of wealth, land ownership, skin colour, and location – in short, a systemic anti-*campesino* (peasant) bias. As such, the pernicious painful repetitions of violence can be transcended, and with the innovative peace process, a prosperous Colombia is a promising possibility.

Yet the act of signing the peace deal is by no means the end. The road ahead is both long, and littered with potential stumbling blocks. A false step could see Colombia forgoing the peace dividend, and tumbling back unto the precarious precipice of a potentially failed state. Although, if anything at this crossroads in Colombian history is certain, it is this: if Colombia can close its veins; and shake off the lingering stings of prying foreign powers, a heartless city elite, and a hyper-politicised discourse of violence – then the country that gave the world the artist Fernando Botero and the Nobel laureate author Gabriel Garcia Marquez, has plenty to offer yet.

A capsule history

Colombian violence reflects a confluence of trends creating the ideal conditions for armed conflict – to better understand the tenets of the peace deal, it helps first to understand a brief overview of Colombian history, and how we have arrived at the present situation.

As a Spanish colony, the area that is now Colombia existed under the broadly feudal rule of the Viceroys. Alongside its neighbouring countries, Colombia was a hub for the extraction of raw materials, namely gold, to be exported to the Iberian Peninsula. Bogotá, the present day capital of Colombia, was the seat of power for the colony of New Granada, covering much of the north of the continent, and the port city of Cartagena was a bustling hub for trans-Atlantic trade. Beyond these nodal points, Colombia was primarily an agrarian society, wherein large Spanish-descended landowners would control vast *haciendas* (rural estates), and had near-total control over the campesinos working their land. Society was also heavily racially segregated, with white Europeans and their direct descendants firmly at the top of the hierarchy, natives and Afro-Colombians at the bottom, and all shades of *mestizo* in-between. Such was the condition of those at the bottom, that not only did their skin colour prevent them ever ascending social ranks, native communities would also be forced into either paying a heavy tithe on top of taxes, or endure forced labour, sometimes both. Whilst this state of racial hegemony caused some amount of disquiet, both between the Spanish governors and the Catholic crown of Castile, the latter of which being concerned for the preservation of indigenous civilisations, and also between the indigenous and/or black populations and their controllers. No such conflict, however, reached the height of Tupac Amaru's 1572 insurrection in the south of the continent, due both to the geographical diversity of the nation, and its role as a focal point for governance.

Short of iterative failed attempts at liberalising the economy, the first of which being by the Bourbon monarchy of Charles VII, Colombia's relation to the rest of the world had been remarkably constant. Namely, it functioned solely as a tribute region to Spain, and was forbidden to engage in international trade with anywhere other than via Spain. This all changed following Napoleon's conquest of the then bankrupt Iberian Peninsula at the turn of the nineteenth century. Despite facing considerable resistance, small *juntas* took advantage of the vacuum in governance to begin appropriating the tools of government for themselves – from forging illegal trade relations with other powers of the day, to securing a monopoly of force from the remnants of Spanish rule. Simon Bolívar, an ambitious aristocrat from modern day Venezuela, and his comrade, the liberal Francisco de Paula Santander, won over a sufficiently large force to topple the Viceroy governance in 1819, overseeing the establishment of the republic of New Granada. As a resourceful demagogue, capable of winning over forces on his route to victory, Bolívar cemented into the Latin American narrative the concept of a *caudillo*, a charismatic leader, typically backed by armed forces, who will either challenge the status quo, or demand special concessions from governing forces. Most caudillos were ideologically ambiguous, or forged their ideologies *a posteri-*

ori to justify their actions, yet in Bolívar's case, his demands for a strong, military-led Pan-American government with close ties to the Church and little regard for popular democracy were very clear – thus leading to him being considered the first conservative caudillo of Colombia. Whilst the name and figure of Bolívar carries significant symbolic weight across the lands for whom he was *el libererador*, the man himself was ostracised shortly after securing independence, and he died whilst making his way into exile, his dream of creating a Pan-American superpower already ruined.

As an independent state, Colombia emerged governed by the Spanish-descended oligarchy, now serving themselves, as opposed to the crown. Not long into the life of the young republic, two parties emerged; the Conservatives, founded by the Catholic church, with a programme of upholding public morality and providing a secure state with a privileged position for the ecclesiastical elite and large landowners; and the Liberals, who, on paper at least, supported the ideas of free trade, reduced taxation, freedom of expression, heightened property rights, and a backed currency. With respect to the Liberal party, we are to understand Liberal more in its traditional sense – the Manchesterian school of Smith and Mill, grounded in the individualistic property theorisations of Locke, as opposed to the more communitarian Liberalism sometimes attributed to Rousseau. The members of these parties were chosen from amongst the same social strata, and their style of governance was largely similar, save for disagreements about the role of the Church in the state, and the issue of currency backing. Indeed, any genuine changes in governing practice would truly only be evident in large settlements, with the broadly feudal rural population existing outside of governmental reach.

Despite their similarities, as many as sixty-three civil wars have been fought in Colombia's short history, most of which between the two dominant parties. Despite the frequency of the said civil wars, there is only one here worth drawing attention to – the War of a Thousand Days at the turn of the twentieth century, a war largely flamed by the Conservative's party's policy to allow unbacked paper currency, hence making Colombia less attractive to foreign investors. Not only was this the longest of South America's civil wars, under the leadership of Raphael Uribe Uribe, a Liberal caudillo, Colombia saw the emergence guerrilla warfare as a tactic in civil conflict. Whilst this tactic was swiftly abandoned, after Uribe noticed the threat that arming campesinos in a manner far from the traditional pitched battle format posed to the ruling hegemony of both sides, the war had a number more far reaching effects. Notably, it took place at a time when Colombia was negotiating the constructing of a trans-oceanic canal in the region of Panama, on the Latin American Isthmus (the narrow strip conjoining North and South America). Seizing on the weakness of the Colombian state as it suppressed the sizeable rebellion, Theodore Roosevelt supported a small uprising in the province of Panama, and prevented the Colombian army from fighting said uprising by positioning a portion of the US navy off the coast at Urabá. Having succeeded in toppling the governmental representatives in Panama City, the rebels then sent an envoy to negotiate the construction of the canal in Washington. However, whilst they were still in transit, the USA formally recognised Panama as an independent country, and the chief engineer of the canal as its representative – persuading him to sign over complete ownership to the USA. Whilst this clear breach of the spirit of the Monroe doctrine is only one of many in Latin American history, it went a long way to seed the germ of mistrust among Colombians for their powerful 'big brother'. Finally, the War of a Thousand Days holds a particular significance in forging peace. The Liberals did not lay down their arms as a consequence of outright military defeat. Rather, they surrendered in return both for secret monetary payments, and for the implementation of the reforms that they craved. As Charles Bergquist notes, in securing their reforms, the Liberals lost the war, yet won the peace. Hence the importance implementing acutely needed reforms holds in the present peace deal. Following the end of this conflict, Colombia enjoyed nearly half a century of relative peace, known as the 'dance of the millions' for its prosperity. That said, the Liberals secured their reforms largely through persuading the population that history was with them -yet, given the fall of the Berlin wall and the implosion of the Soviet Union, the guerrillas of today face a far larger task to do the same. A point that appears to be lost on the ELN, yet well received by the FARC, who have transformed their rhetoric away from overt Leninism, into supporting a European style social democracy.

Yet the millions did not dance for all – the coffee and banana export boom that fuelled a growth spurt in the Colombian economy served predominantly to fuel land and wealth concentration. Moreover, it was impossible to halt this process due to the chronic weakness of the Colombian labour movement. The paroxysm of this class conflict can be found in the 1928 *Bananeros* massacre. Thousands of United Fruit workers and their families convened upon the Urabán city of Cienagá, to protest for better working conditions, pay, fair weights and measurements, and the right to be paid in cash, rather than coupons for the company stores. For fear that the protest would be a threat to the status quo, the Colombian army killed hundreds of workers and their families in the crowd. This event earns a traumatic and pivotal scene in Marquez's masterpiece, *One Hundred Years of Solitude*, where the event was followed by unanimous silence. Yet whilst, as Luis Alberto Restrepo outlined, violence in Colombia is met with a public outcry that is only ever short lived, there was a charismatic young lawyer who refused to let the event blow over – Jorge Eliecer Gaitán, who toured much of Colombia, rallying the pueblo to resist such abuses.

Gaitán sparked an immensely popular movement of left-liberalism that gathered momentum from the late 1920s onwards. However, despite his colossal support base, the *Gaitanismo* movement was forever at odds with the established rulers of the Liberal Party, who challenged him by persistently blocking him from running for important offices, undermining him through their control over the press, and even violently suppressing his supporters. Despite this, he ran as an independent candidate, split the vote, and succeeded in become the irresistible favourite for the 1950 election. Had he triumphed in securing the election and implementing his radical land reform policies, the Colombian political situation would likely be far more favourable today. However, in April 1948, on the same day he was set to meet a young Cuban lawyer named Fidel Castro, he was gunned down on a street in Bogotá. Before the assassin could put names to the "powerful, dangerous forces" under whose command he operated, he was lynched by a mob of *Gaitánistas*.

Upon the confirmation of Gaitán's death a few hours later, waves of low level violence and looting broke out across Bogotá, known as the *Bogotazo*. Given that the city was then hosting the ninth Conference of American Nations, the Conservative administration saw fit to violently repress the Bogotazo, which it broadly succeeded in doing.

However, this chain of repressions and reactive rebellions sparked the chaotic period of internal conflict known in Colombia simply as *La Violencia*. The subsequent decade saw Liberal campesinos take up arms against Conservative campesinos and vice versa in a dirty war that cost the lives of over 200,000 people. Yet in this mad world of death, blood, and fire – new ideological stances muscled their way into the fray. Armed groups, either seeking to seed class consciousness amongst warring campesinos, or composed of intellectuals and students inspired by the Soviet Union, began to gather in strength and momentum, targeting rancheros, caciques, and members of the military. This coincided with a growing paranoia surrounding communism in the USA. Hence, to investigate the threat, the US tasked General William P. Yarborough with deciding the course of action that the US should take to secure a favourable result. Yarborough delivered Plan Lazo, which contains the chilling suggestions involving:

> "clandestine execution of plans developed by the United States government towards defined objectives in the political, economic, and military fields" including "paramilitary, sabotage, and/or

terrorist activities against communist
proponents. It should be backed by
the United States".

The plan was met by a boost for in funding for the
Colombian military, and the provision of weapons
and advisors. Whilst this report indicates the involvement the USA has in the genesis of the paramilitary forces that would plague Colombian society
right through to the present. Little did the government know that further intensification of the
conflict would only spur the growth of armed radical campesinos by cracking open a powder-keg of
anti-elite sentiment. La Violencia formally came
to end with the 1957 National Front agreement,
where the Conservative and Liberal parties signed
to share power through mixed cabinets and a pres-
idency that alternated between parties every five
years, thus allowing them to combine forces to
tackle the threat posed by guerrilla campesino groups.

The newly unified Colombian military worked
with local paramilitaries to eradicate remaining armed
groups of leftist campesinos – who were now inspired by the success of the Cuban revolution. In
the Tolima village of Mantequila lived 48 armed
campesinos fitting this description. In May 1964,
16,000 Colombian soldiers supported by a fleet

of US provided B-26 bombers launched an offensive to annihilate the guerrillas. Not only did all 48 avoid either capture or death, they even held a conference during the offensive, where they decided to pursue guerrilla tactics to secure agrarian reform. So goes the remarkable foundation story of the FARC. The group then went on to launch a bottom up revolutionary programme, wherein they recruited from, and were sustained by, disaffected campesinos on a local level. Other guerrilla movements emerged at a similar time, most notable were the ELN – a liberation-theology driven collective of middle class intellectuals and students, and M-19, a group comprised of the eclectic melange of Marxists, Liberals, and Conservatives – the latter of which being disaffected by the undemocratic nature of the National Front. Given the threat these groups posed to the effective management of businesses and estates, paramilitary forces emerged as a counterweight to the guerrillas, acting on behalf of landowners, the army, and corporations – all of whom feared for the effective operation of their work, and the security of their property.

Violence between these armed actors originally functioned at a low level; guerrillas constructed their support base in areas where the government was weak or absent, paramilitaries attempted to undermine the growth of guerrilla forces, the military sought to reclaim land lost to guerrillas, and the US continued to prop up the Colombian government under the prevalent Cold War mantra. However, approaching the 1980s, a spike in the international cocaine price following a cocaine boom in the USA magnified the scale of the conflict on all sides. The FARC raised considerable amounts of wealth by facilitating and taxing the narcotics trade in areas they controlled, this allowed them to grow both in land conquest and military might. The paramilitaries also enjoyed the drugs boom, free from the moral constraints of direct implication in the trade, the booming wealth of the drug kingpins provided another lucrative customer for them to serve. A solid wage and the possibility of a short cut to extreme wealth motivated countless poor urban youths to join the private armies of say, Pablo Escobar – frequently in the role of a hitmen for hire, *sicarios*. Whilst the guerrillas fought with the belief that they marched along an inevitable historical progression that would likely not be realised in their lifetimes, sicarios operated under the belief in a fleeting existence coloured by the extremes of the human condition, from which they are liberated only in reward after death. The paramilitaries and the guerrillas were not the only actors to expand in this period of intensifying violence – the military and intelligence services enjoyed support from President Reagan, under the double pronged attack of a 'War on Drugs' and a continuing desire to undermine leftist forces in Latin America. With the stakes rising for all parties involved, it would seem that something had to buckle.

In response to the changing nature of the violence – towards total war – the government and the FARC sought to make peace. In early 1984, the FARC sought to distance themselves from armed struggle by signing a bilateral ceasefire with the government, and instead lent their weight to a leftist alliance party known as *Union Patriotica* (UP). In its first election, 1986, the UP enjoyed considerable success; enough, that is, to threaten the recently separated Liberal and Conservative parties in open elections. Consequently, as the new administration of President Turbay took the opportunity to increase the creation of paramilitary groups so as to annihilate the UP via a dirty war; over the latter half of the 1980s, the UP suffered a political genocide in which over 2000 of its members, including two presidential candidates, three elected mayors and four elected congressmen, were killed – henceforth gutting the UP, and preventing it from being a viable political force. The killings were carried out by paramilitary forces, often with the compliance of the Colombian army. Indeed, it later transpired that the command to assassinate the UP presidential candidate Bernardo Jaramillo Ossa in 1989 came from the head of internal intelligence, Alberto Romero.

Following the failure of the UP experiment, the FARC returned to partaking in armed struggle in their rural strongholds. The 1990s saw a peaking of the FARC powerbase, they controlled almost half of Colombian territory, undertook large, often successful, offensives against military bases and small cities, and developed increasingly brutal tactics of securing their goals. This involved an upsurge in kidnappings to fund their programme, kidnappings which started by targeting the loved ones of urban elites, yet descending into simply stopping cars on the street to kidnap their inhabitants. Famously, they kidnapped the liberal-reform minded French-Colombian presidential candidate Ingrid Bettencourt – and held her in the jungle for six years. Both for the traumatic physical and psychological effects that kidnappings have on their victims, and the power that their targets had over the forming of public opinion, cost the FARC the little respect they may have held in Colombian discourse. Far more paradoxical than the pseudo-class warfare entailed in the practice of kidnapping was the FARC's programme of protecting their land through land mining. Whilst the process of mining the surrounding regions may have been effective – the primary victims of the exercise are the campesinos that the FARC exist to protect. Despite – or indeed because of – these practices, the FARC continued to consolidate power, until the US embassy predicted that the FARC would take power over the nation shortly after the millennium. This intensification of guerrilla warfare occurred whilst the Colombian government faced an internal war with powerful drug kingpins resisting extradition – most famously, Pablo Escobar and his Medellín cartel. The resultant explosion of urban violence caused Colombian cities to emerge as global murder hotspots, with gang warfare frequently being manifest in car bombs, public assassinations, and massacres. In this period, the Colombian murder rate spiked to over 70 people per 100,000, for comparison, the Latin American average hovered around thirteen, and the Canadian figure was a mere two. Moreover, displacement reached a scale not before seen, with 150,000 – 200,000 people being forced from their homes by the violence each year. In 1991, as violence was reaching a fever pitch, a collection of public intellectuals in Colombia, including Gabriel Garcia Marquez and Fernando Botero, constructed a letter to the guerrillas pleading that they refrain from violent struggle and attempt to regain the sympathy of the intelligentsia through pursuing democratic means to change. Whilst the guerrillas responded amiably, claiming that violent struggle is the only option afforded to them by government practices, the 'letter of the intellectuals' captured the hearts of the Colombian public, and the attention of the world, and altered attitudes to the changing nature of the violence.

The scourge of narco-trafficking violence began to peter out towards the end of the millennium, first with the 1991 constitution enshrining protection from extradition to the US, the 1993 killing of Escobar, and the violent dismantling of the Calí cartel. That is not to say that narco-trafficking gangs disappeared, but rather they merged with the faceless web of organised crime in Colombia, and took on a more ambiguous relationship with the government – one of underhand political pressure, rather than open warfare. The aforementioned constitution of 1991 deserves special attention, whilst it was openly abused by subsequent politicians, and was followed by two decades of brutal violence, it set the ground for a governmental position dedicated to the provision of peace, and the eradication of social discrimination. Ana María Bejarno described it in 1999 as "a constitution for angels" – as such, it is not means imminently realistic, rather is an ideal towards which Colombian democracy slowly marches.

The 2000s witnessed firstly the implementation of Plan Colombia, President Clinton's initiative supposedly aimed at stemming the flow of narcotics into the USA. The plan contained a collection of policy implementations to be funded - varying from constructive pledges to reduce unemployment (then around 20%), pragmatic pledges such as the modernisation of the Colombian military, to questionable pledges to privatise the nation's healthcare system, and implement "severe austerity and adjustment measures". The latter being particularly peculiar due to Colombia having endured a decade of austerity prior to the plan – under which un-

employment had ballooned, state services had col-
lapsed, the national debt had spiked, and the military lacked the funding to appropriately deal with
the conflict. Under Plan Colombia, Colombia enjoyed the choice claim of being the largest recipi-
ent of US military aid, overtaking Israel and Egypt,
and receiving up to $1 billion annually. The ma-
jority of US military aid (around 70%) was spent
on combatting guerrilla forces. As Human Rights/Americas
Watch point out, the US aid was provided with
minimal end-use monitoring. Hence, it was not
unusual for the equipment to be tools in massacres
and other severe human rights abuses. That said,
without the considerable boost provided by Plan
Colombia, it is unlikely the FARC would have been
weakened to the extent they are today.

The election of the Alvaro Uribe in 2002, on a
vehement policy of national security, ushered in a
new dark era of dirty war, notably marred by human rights scandals in the battlefield, paramilitary
corruption scandals in governance, and a toxic sphere
of public discussion - where you are either with
Uribe, or you are guerrilla. Whilst the suppression of pluralist viewpoints, the fermenting of the
myth of pure evil with respect to the guerrillas,
and Uribe's vitriolic campaign against the peace

deal, has no doubt harmed the efforts of those wanting to bring the war to a close through the Havana negotiations, his administration ironically can be credited for changing the security situation so as to make peace possible. With the military becoming better equipped to quash guerrilla warfare, and less concerned about the typical rules of just war, the guerrillas are perhaps more keen than anyone to negotiate a lasting peace that involves their protection. Finally, Uribe's gift to Colombia includes a demonstration of how a demobilisation process should not take place. In 2006, he negotiated the demobilisation of the AUC, a group unifying paramilitaries. Despite his protests about impunity in the present deal, he granted lenient sentences to paramilitary actors in the Colombian conflict, neglected any real attempt at reconciliation, made little to no changes to the social fabric that brought forth paramilitary groups, did not put the peace deal to a referendum, and then undertook a programme of denying the continued existence of the paramilitaries. Consequently, groups comprised of former paramilitary leaders and members now run groups fulfilling the same role as paramilitary groups and have a similar sway in local and national governance – only they are now not called paramilitaries. They refer to themselves under a variety of names – such as the potent *Los Urabaneous* and *Los Rastrojos* gangs – and are labelled by the government as common bandits, despite their continued commitment to political action and social cleansing. The government frequently cycles through labels for these groups, with BaCrim being a name that has stuck in the public consciousness; however, English Language newspapers operating in Colombia opt for the secure name of 'paramilitary successor groups'. Whilst some of these groups are vying for belligerent status, and hence a place at the negotiating table – whatever claim they may have formerly been able to make towards being a political agent (namely, fulfilling the role of the state in enforcing property laws) has been lost as a consequence of their peace deal. In much the same respect, FARC guerrillas who refuse to put down arms, as is feared of the fifth front, or who otherwise join forces with other armed actors, can expect the same relegation to non-belligerent common criminal status following a just implementation of the peace deal.

The history of Colombia is a history of violence. Violence that has far more to do with the chronic social injustices that abound in Colombian society; inequality of wealth, land displacement, political participation, and electoral fraud to name a few; than any supposed violent temperament in the Colombian people. The bleak picture painted above pertains only to understanding the peace deal. The balanced reality, however, consists of a nation with unparalleled diversity. A nation in which one can find three forested mountain ranges, two expansive coastlines, and vast swathes of the Amazon plains, not to mention a plethora of ecological niches, such as the Savannah plains of the Wayuu people. The changing security situation in Colombia, coupled with a remarkably well educated populace, has seen Colombia become a regional hotspot for a fledgling Latin American IT industry. Moreover, the country has given birth to countless exemplars of the human race – from the dynamic Gaitán, to the international greats of the artistic world such as Debora Arango, Marquez, and Botero; even to the thousands of honest people who stand up the offensive injustices that purvey in society to this day, in the capacity of lawyers, trade unionists, human rights activists, academics, journalists, and charity workers – all of whom face ugly chances of survival in their profession, yet continue operating under the belief that even if the work they do costs them their lives, it may alleviate the suffering of their compatriots and the generations that follow them. Finally, Colombia is a hotbed for internal and international cultural developments – from the vibrant Salsa sounds of La-33 or the Guayácan Orchestra, the electro-tropical beats of Bomba Estereo, the world renowned Shakira, the artsy Monsieur Periné, the fascinating prints, new and old, that line the walls of city galleries, and above all the dream like narratives of the magical realist authors.

The blame game

The average Colombian, and, indeed, for a different reason, the average Westerner uninterested in the political nuances at the butt end of the supply chain for the cheap products lining their homes, has been fed a politically deliberate picture of an embattled government at war with leftist guerrillas, narco-guerrillas, or narco-terrorists (depending on which 'War on...' is in vogue in the USA). The truth, as it has a habit of being, is far more complex.

Firstly, the conflict has been fought between a complex web of actors; the guerrillas, the military, the paramilitaries, paramilitary-successor groups, and irregular groups of criminal bandits (BaCrim). Whilst the guerrillas are certainly no angels, they are responsible for around only 20% of human rights abuses – and of these abuses, they typically follow financial motives – such as kidnapping family members of the Colombian elite, and 'taxing' foreign corporations for extracting Colombian wealth. The remainder of offences pertain to the military, and the remnants of the frequently government-linked yet allegedly non-existent paramilitary groups. Offences by these groups typically involve the massacre and domination of civilians deemed sympathetic to guerrillas (whom they were not above dressing up as guerrillas, to provide 'false positives' towards body count targets), violence towards trade unionists, and forced displacement to provide cheap ranching land. Perhaps their most perturbing practice is 'social cleansing'; the eradication of 'defective' humans, typically considered the homeless, prostitutes, leftists, and homosexuals. Unfortunately, no sector of society is immune to witnessing this practice, and the threat of being caught in the crossfire is startlingly present. One friend recounts stories of armed men, with chained Pitbulls at hand, running metal bars along chain link fences to alert the barrio to their presence – effectively causing a lockdown of an area, and stoking unimaginable fear in all caught outside. Whilst, as journalist Adriaan Anselma elicits, the penetration of dubiously-linked people into the upper echelons of the political class remains a concern. The Colombian state has been quite effective at cutting its ties with the paramilitaries, especially following the para-politics scandal of 2006, which implicated 139 Colombian congressmen as being in the pockets of the paramilitaries. Consequently, despite still enjoying financial support from large land-owners, Colombian businesses, and multi-national corporations (including fruit giants, Chiquita), the paramilitary groups can be considered criminal groups, and targeted as such. Whilst still too keen on neo-Nazi thuggery, governance by extortion, and international drug trafficking to be considered common criminals, they are far enough away from political debate to require a special place at the peace table.

This disassociation allows for the innovate step by the government in accepting that they too have blood on their hands, thus not rendering this a peace deal of domination, but one that champions justice. By accepting their responsibility for past crimes, state actors can be tried in the special transitional justice courts alongside guerrillas, and then experience a lenient community-service based punishment. This step is vital in the process of reconciliation, as it allows for the dissolution of what are referred to as 'hereditary hatreds', the generations-old bad blood between organised Colombian groups, are necessary.

Securing a *sí*

Yet the special courts of transitional justice, for all their merits, rely first on Colombians opting to sign the peace deal in the forthcoming election. Herein lies the problem of guerrilla perception. How do you convince a public fed on anti-guerrilla vitriol, that revenge should not be exacted upon the war criminals at whose hands they have suffered, and that instead they will enjoy 'punishments' such as mine clearance, forestry management, and infrastructure maintenance? The answer, of course, is with remarkable difficultly.

However, the fault lines of opinion do not lie where one may expect. Those most hostile to a lack of retributive justice are often those with the smallest stake in the violence; be they the urban middle class, wealthy landowners, or citizens from areas of relative peace. Those often ardently in favour of the signing of the deal are victims' groups, intellectuals, and campesinos from areas of turmoil. It is those who have either had to bury their love ones well before their rightful time, those who have looked beyond the propaganda machine of the regrettable former Uribe government, and those who want little more than a definitive end to the political violence.

What hope does the government have of overcoming decades of propaganda on behalf of the *Uribistas*, and the present reactionary wave demanding harsher conditions? Fortunately, quite a lot, whilst the polls have been erratic and unpredictable, a Brexit style 'no' vote is quite unlikely. However, the reason for this does not lie in rational public discourse and national consensus, but in the lingering problem of electoral fraud. Anselma notes that around 20% of municipalities where the referendum will be held are at considerable risk of manipulation, this will likely be enough to swing a majority. Elections in Colombia are still far from 'free and fair', but rather they are controlled by regional oligarchic *jefes* (sometimes known as *gamonals* or *caciques*), who guarantee results in return for political favours. An interesting array of tactics are used to ensure these results are secured, from simple vote-buying, to tactical 'accidents' in registration, such as the reversal of maternal and paternal surnames, which prevent people from voting. In sum, elections typically boil down to the decisions of around two dozen families. Of these families, the Santos clan, to which President Santos belongs, is one of, if not the, most powerful. Consequently, Santos can bank on the support of the bulk of these clans, unlike Alvaro Uribe, the former president and key voice in opposing the deal, who now acts as something of an oligarchic pariah.

Whilst it should be added that this system of vote manipulation by no means accounts for every vote, in tight-run elections, it will likely be sufficient to tip the balance. The same fraud-ridden electoral machine that allowed Santos to be elected despite a negative approval rating, will allow the peace deal to go through without hindrance.

The thorny task of implementation

The key to a meaningful peace is not the collection of well-intentioned airs emitted from a clockwork of committees, sub-commissions, and international observers; but the efficacy and speed with which the Colombian state can enact the crucial reforms promised. Whilst the sclerotic ailments such as tax reform (around the equivalent of 25% of Colombia's GDP is stashed in overseas tax havens), racism, and structural inequality, will take a long time to be subordinated sufficiently to be squeezed out of the system – the government has a very real opportunity to make headway in the crucial projects of land restitution and victim reparation.

The importance of land restitution cannot be understated; almost 6 million people, around 15%

of the population, have been forced from their homes by conflict. Most of the time, these have been campesinos, whose clearance has paved the way to increase the holdings of large landowners. These people have then either taken refuge in city slums, or attempted to settle virgin territory: both scenarios conjure a plethora of pitfalls for the new settlers. To historically contextualise the point of land conflict – effectively every major conflict in Colombian history since the civil war at the turn of the century, has been about the increasing concentration of land; from Gaitán's popular movements, under his mantra of *"no soy un hombre, soy un pueblo"* ("I am not a man, but the 'people'"), from the 1920s until his assassination in 1948, to the rural guerrilla movements of the FARC, ELN, and their since demobilised equivalents.

From having worked with a handful of lawyers tasked with land restitution, one thing can be assured: it is a tangled and thorny mess. Attempts to meet government targets for returned land are consistently pitiful – and not for lack of trying. Instead, those working on the task face a three pronged challenge.

Firstly, they are often dealing with claims that date back decades, wherein the present occupiers of the land may have little or no idea of the brutal circumstances under which their property was appropriated. Then there is the issue of land titles – campesinos may have worked their family's land for centuries, yet, quite understandably, a community of, say, indigenous people, will at no point have felt the compulsion to actually acquire title deeds for the land that their family has worked for time immemorial. Here we must remember that for swathes of isolated Colombia, generations of families may have existed without any contact from the state - save for being pillaged by the occasional passing army. As such, as an overworked and underpaid civil rights lawyer, it can be impossible to make a meaningful claim when the only legal evidence you have to put against a powerful landowner, say, Colombia's oxymoronically named nation oil company Ecopetrol (another financier of the paramilitaries), is the assurance by an ageing world-weary slum dweller that his family used to work the land from the river there, to that tree there, beyond which the property of his long since massacred neighbour's family began. Finally, political intimidation is not dead. Campesinos trying to reclaim their former lands are often publicly humiliated as 'liars' if their case does not succeed, and those who are trying to make their claims are often targeted by the charmless paramilitary death-squads working on behalf of the landowners.

As such, the Colombian government can reasonably progress in one of two ways: either they can hurl a bounty of resources behind the process of restitution, including protection of claimants, and bending interpretations of the law in their favour; or they can seek alternative settlement programmes in government controlled lands. Despite the hanging spectre of ecological damage, the latter may be preferable. For it involves stepping on fewer toes, it can be implemented quicker, and, as Donny Meertens notes, given the brutality of their expulsion, many victims – especially female victims – do not want to return to where they were expelled from, but instead would either like to settle somewhere new, or be aided in increasing their financial independence in the cities. Victim reparations face similar problems, especially in discerning who is and who isn't a victim. Here, sticky legal definitions should be avoided for victimhood – victims of the conflict are diverse, and include in some way the bulk of the country. As such, victim reparation should really be seen as government reform, especially rural reform. Herein lies the importance of projects such as crop substitution (to provide financially realistic alternatives to growing coca), infrastructure projects, and education. The ambitions of the peace process have all been promising to this end, yet these are all promises the government has iteratively made decades before, and come up short. This time there needs to be no roads that take 30 years to build, no farmers who find the promised crops for which they uprooted their coca never appearing, or appearing only to be latterly fumigated by coca spraying projects, or for that matter, appearing and being cultivated, only for them to rot in the ground because the promised road connecting them to the market was never built.

Effective rural reform will starve guerrillas and paramilitaries of their support base – often people only join due to a desperate lack of opportunity, or to escape some other source of violence, rather than an ardent ideological stance. As a journalist put it to me, "you can either take over from your poor as shit abusive father's farm and die of malnutrition, or you can go with the group that has motorcycles and gets laid... you go for the getting laid option".

However, even if these reforms can be effective, there still remains the problem of how to reinte-

grate around 7,000 demobilised guerrillas into society, and prevent them from drifting into other
armed groups. Firstly, it's unclear whether the majority of guerrillas will want to be 're-integrated'.
On the one hand, there is the argument that to be
able to attain a decent job, reclaim their reproduc-
tive rights (guerrillas are not supposed to be parents), and to leave the precarious existence of liv-
ing between forest camps, awaiting the likely fate
of being mutilated by paramilitaries; many who
joined only through a lack of security or realistic opportunities will take that chance with both
hands. After all, as a consequence of a sincere in-
sistence of a holistic education, former FARC fighters will be brilliantly equipped for most jobs. Yet,
in contrast, many will also be unwilling to leave
their comrades in the jungle, and enter into a world
that has been conditioned to be hostile to them.
The latter stance has added potency when consid-
ering former attempts for the FARC to become a
legitimate political force. Most notably, the political genocide of around 3,000 members of the
FARC-aligned UP party in the early 1980s; a massacre that effectively annihilated what had very quickly
become a powerful political force (and unsurprisingly, a genocide carried out with complicity both

from the elite governing body, and right wing death squads).

To satisfy both of these groups, the government needs to ensure that it provides honest and adequate protection for former guerrillas wishing to re-enter society, public discourse needs to become more commodious to pluralist views that don't treat any movement outside of the oligarchic elite as communist terrorists (community service should probably help this, as should the otherwise unremarkable President Santos' commitment to pluralism), and potential jobs that don't involve a nine-to-five and a mortgage, but complement the romantic lifestyle of former guerrillas. These will firstly include the behemoth task of mine clearance, but can later be extended to programmes such as ecological management. Ultimately, it is necessary that the conditions are created for a peaceful life to be preferable to a life outside the law.

The final major hurdle to successful implementation is the problem of claiming a monopoly of governance for the state. As it stands, considerable swathes of Colombia either have no state presence, and are governed by guerrillas or other armed groups, or the state governs parallel to an armed group – with different issues being resolved by different governing powers. In the first instance, as previously mentioned, the state has often simply never had a true presence in these areas. As such, citizens pay taxes to groups such as the FARC, who, in return, protect them from the various groups that chase after their land or resources; they also effectively govern the area through providing a justice system, infrastructure and healthcare, and often they do a better job than the Bogotá elite, for whom rural Colombia is little more than a frontier playground wherein they can expand their wealth.

The government only has a brief window of protection provided by the UN, after which they will have to govern these areas on their own. However, a weak state presence runs the risk of being overruled by another armed actor, potentially, as one analyst suggested to me, by Colombia's other major guerrilla group, the ELN. However, to put it bluntly, nobody, including the ELN, really has any idea what the ELN intend to do. However, the threat of capture by narco-trafficking paramilitaries is very real, and it should be added (especially by looking at their record with the mining industry), that they aren't shining examples of good governance. The world should fear any group that attempts to kill poverty through killing the poor.

This problem of handing over governance has been exacerbated by a handful of FARC fronts retreating from the seat of power ahead of schedule. This is because, without the promise of armed protection by the larger FARC network (who are almost unanimously holding true to the spirit of the ceasefire), they and their families are effective sitting ducks for groups wishing to stake a claim in the region. For the handover process to be successful, it is imperative once again that a decent degree of protection is provided for those who have laid down their arms, and that the government is able to come good on promises to provide sufficient resources for the project. For this final point, the capricious question of finance needs to be readdressed later.

Ideological self-reflection

Colombian elections have frequently been decided on the guerrilla question. Whether it has been Uribe's potent national security platform in 2002, or Santos' 2010 drive for peace, the focal point of public debate has been how to bring about an end to the war. Consequently, other social debates, such as tackling racial and gender discrimination in Colombia, haven't been topics of burning relevance. Moreover, the possibility for debate has frequently been quelled by the acidic discourse that pits anything opposed to a strict party line as being the talk of guerrillas. With the retreat of guerrillas from the theatre of conflict, a space will be cleared for elections to be run on maladies that have long afflicted the Colombian people.

The need for diverse public debate is vast. For the bulk of Colombian history, leading parties have been separated by little more than their names, and their relationship with the Catholic church. As such, problems such as an insulting minimum wage (around 75 pence per hour), punitive trade deals, and endemic corruption, have persisted without serious outcry. With the conflict's monopoly of news coverage coming to end, the space can be cleared for a genuine public redress of these issues. The consequence of this will either be the inception of a genuine opposition between the leading parties, as they each opt for different sides on the debate, or the rolling aside of the traditional power blocs to permit representation by fringe parties. In the case of the preferable latter, the consequence may even be the disintegration of the traditional oligarchy.

To change public debate is certainly not a process that can occur immediately; everyone educated publicly up until the early 1990s will have had their schooling provided the Catholic church (who, in turn, form the crux of support for the Conservative party); and additionally, only with the recent rise of relative peace has the space for academic freedom to pursue ideas outside of traditional hard-line economic liberalism been provided. By consequence, it will be the generation of elites educated on Keynes and Marx as much as they are on Smith and Hayek who will have the potential to bring about serious alternatives to the dominant neo-liberal economic paradigm adopted by the bulk of governing powers. Whatever one's views may be on the ideal system of economic governance, few can doubt the importance of a genuine opposition, so as to curb the greatest excesses of a unitary system.

Equally important in the social sphere is the fact that the current generation are the first to be connected to the global community via the internet. The filter of new ideas into society that results from this is the uprooting of the social hegemony formerly held by the Catholic church. As a result, questions regarding the fixity of gender roles, the moral worth of deviant sexual orientations, and the validity of a racial hierarchy are being raised. Whilst issues of racial and gender equality are not new to Colombian society, for they have long formed a significant portion of the FARC's political agenda, the fibre-optic driven arrival of said views has accelerated the debate. The permeation of these arguments into public discourse has already been evident; namely in the inclusion of gender and LGBT based sub commissions reviewing the details of the peace agreement through a liberation-focused lens.

The advantages of social liberalisation are three-fold. Firstly, for what is hopefully the majority of readers, equality regardless of gender, race, orientation or any other arbitrary facet of the human composition, is intrinsically desirable in almost any society. Yet in addition to this, social equality will also work to cut the feed of young people entering armed groups; either through a rationale grounded in escaping a life underlined by domestic service, and likely blotted with gender based violence; or through a commitment to machismo culture, leading down-at-heel youths to seek the romantic, and potentially lucrative (if they join paramilitary successor groups), life of an armed combatant. Finally, the added gender perspective allows for the war to be understood as a simply masculine affair. Since the transition to guerrilla based insurgency in the early twentieth century, and the rise of 'dirty war', the Colombian conflict has been anything but entirely male, with gender based violence frequently acting as a tool for social domination and terror creation. In accepting the gender component of the violence, greater legitimacy can be granted to the numerous women's victim groups existing in civil society – without simply labelling them as being too cosy to guerrillas, and hence fair game violent repression.

Social liberation, however, has a considerable way to go. One need only to listen to the words filing the Reggaeton tracks thumping from bars, clubs, cars and taxis to find that regressive social attitudes are still rife, even amongst the youth. Regardless of whether listeners actually take heed to lyrics declaring toxic axioms suggesting all women to be sluts, clearly the lack of ostensible outcry points to a degree of social complicity. Moreover, outside of the cities, the idea that a woman's sole purpose is as a home maker still holds strong; with few opportunities for fiscal independence existing beyond pitifully paid domestic work. Indeed, such is the lack of gender advancement in rural Colombia, that the possibility of financial self-sustenance is often cited as a reason why forcibly displaced women wish to remain on the fringes of cities, rather than returning to an onerous life of domestic docility in the countryside.

The all-too visible hand

US involvement in Colombian affairs is nothing new; indeed, under the guise of the Monroe doctrine, the totality of the Latin American continent has been the battleground for US interests for the majority of the respective republics' histories. The cause for US involvement in Colombia is clear; Colombia is a nation with bountiful natural wealth. As such, one needn't be surprised to find Colombia as having been on the receiving end of iterative US interventions under a variety of guises, whether it is Theodore Roosevelt's backing of a Panamanian independence movement in order to secure favourable (indeed, dominant) contractual terms for an inter-oceanic canal, the Cold War, the War on Drugs, or the War on Terror, the list goes on. More recently, the US's hand is even evident in forcing the neo-liberal 'opening' reforms as preconditions for military aid in 'Plan Colombia'. It is unsurprising therefore, that until 2004, the US embassy in Bogotá was the largest such embassy in the world. Moreover, the cynic would argue that it is no coincidence that areas of intense historic violence, such as Urabá, Barrancabermeja, and Guajira, are also areas of considerable US interest in resources: in these cases, bananas, oil, and coal respectively. Regarding the US's drive for such reforms, whether the causal link starts with a desire for multinationals to be able to negotiate with a precarious state and employ a desperate population, or whether a desperate population and a precarious state arise from multinational presence, is difficult to ascertain. What is clear is that, as with countless cases the world over, the two forces march in step.

Claims that US involvement in Colombia has been uniformly negative abound in the literature surrounding the conflict. They are, however, patently untrue. Firstly, were it not for the military aid provided to quash the revolutionary left under Clinton's 'Plan Colombia', working of course in conjunction with former President Uribe's disregard for the rule of law, then the FARC would have either claimed a national victory, leading to a likely

Chavista style of governance (i.e. anti-western and heavily populist), or the FARC would at least not be negotiating from the position of weakness they find themselves in for the present peace deal. Moreover, when US military aid isn't trifled away on socially destructive projects - such as crop fumigation – or for that matter simply 'disappeared' in the machinery of Colombian governance, then it has successfully worked to the end outlined under Plan Colombia to modernise the Colombian armed forces, and hence haste the arrival of an end to the stalemate. To complement the knowledge acquired from decades of experience in fighting the organised network operating under the surface of society, the Colombian army now has US equipped units, with specialist training and decent pay – a far cry from the conscription-led ill-equipped forces that dominated governmental efforts over previous decades.

All the same, the rush of US funding under both the Clinton and Bush administrations, which flitted between $350 million and $1 billion annually, sent in order to prop up the Colombian military, has had a number of detrimental effects to Colombian society; effects that make the Colombian government wary of accepting financial support in the implementation of the peace deal. With respect to the military nature of the funding, the key issue fermenting disquiet was the lack of end-usage monitoring provided – an issue particularly pertinent in the elite Mobile Brigades, who, whilst they were supposedly trained in respecting human rights, are noted by Humans Rights Watch as inflicting a multitude of egregious offences onto rural populations. Such was the perversity of the usage of US supplied weapons that, after the penetration of paramilitary groups into public offices was revealed, congress blocked further spending boosts on the grounds of funding terrorism.

The social qualm of accepting financial support from international backers such as the USA, IMF, EU, and the World Bank, often come with conditions that are questionably beneficial to the Colombian people. One example is a deal cut under the neo-liberal 'opening' of Colombia in the early 1990s, where protectionist measures sustaining the Colombian oil industry were disbanded, allowing for oil to be extracted entirely by foreign countries, shipped to the USA for refinement, and then sold back to Colombia at market prices (albeit, prices that would make European consumers' eyes bulge). Other examples are the iterative demands for strict austerity measures coupled with 'structural adjustments' including privatisation – famously of the health service, exacted by foreign powers unto the Colombian government. Whatever one's views may be on the merits and demerits of the political economy entailed by the Washington consensus; as a matter of governmental accountability and legitimacy, decisions regarding the economic governance of a nation are better made from within its borders.

Finally, foreign financial involvement in Colombia has frequently been ring-fenced for the behemoth task of constricting the flow of narcotics, namely cocaine and marijuana, to US shores. The funding has invariably been to tackle the problem through the fallible method of military force, rather than addressing the conditions that co-opt Colombians into the financial necessity of coca production, and US citizens into ceaselessly demanding the product. Consequently, the funding is frequently channelled to efforts such as crop fumigation, which serves only to attack the lowest rung of the narcotic supply chain – not only by driving growers into further economic desperation, but also the simultaneous harms of ecological damage, and the destruction of legitimate crops. All of which serves to further alienate the campesino class from their central government, and often drives their sympathies towards the guerrilla or paramilitary groups who protect them from these regressive policies; policies which, it should be added, have done nothing to stem the flow of narcotics into the USA over the past few decades, indeed, 2016 has been a year of record coca production in Colombia, much as similar policies saw Afghani poppy production enjoy an equivalent peak harvest in 2015.

It does not take a huge deductive leap to accept Bergquist's diagnosis of the repeated failures of US counter-narcotic work; either US law makers are systematically irrational and unintelligent in their construction of counter-narcotics support, a premise difficult to accept, or they have an ulterior motive supporting the sustenance of a thriving drug trade and the suppression of supplier nations. Whether it is the labour force of a sizeable group of incarcerated youths comprised disproportionately of ethnic minorities, or the strategic weakness of governments in resource hubs that is desired by US policymakers, what is clear is that on almost all counts, the War on Drugs has been disastrous for Colombia, and should make them cautious of further influxes of US finance.

To rephrase an argument made countless times before, a bilateral legalisation, regulation, and taxation of the narcotics trade, as is the case with alcohol and tobacco, would undermine the vast majority of problems the trade imbues. It would remove the need for powerful illegal organisations to refine and transport the drugs, it would enhance the physical and financial security of the growers, it would add countless millions to public coffers – which could be devoted to treating the conditions that drive people into usage and production, and could fund rehabilitation treatment – and would ultimately provide a far safer product for the end user. Bar some promising movements amongst a handful of lawmakers – some of which in Latin America, such as Uruguay's legalisation of marijuana, and the project by Colombian Senator, Juan Manuel Galán (son of the charismatic former presidential candidate Luis Carlos Galán, who was assassinated in 1990 at Pablo Escobar's command) to legalise coca for medicinal purposes – world leaders continue to reject meaningful liberalisations of drug policies.

Whilst the developmental worth of financial involvement from foreign governmental agents has been ambiguous, the involvement of foreign firms enjoying low costs and light labour regulations has lacked the same ambiguity, and not for positive reasons. The classic argument can be raised that the presence of multinational corporations such as Chiquita or ExxonMobil provides the Colombian populace with employment and foreign direct investment (FDI) and jobs that otherwise would not exist – and also that through substituting imports for home-grown industrial outputs (import substitution development, an alternative to free trade), Colombia has previously tailed off from global competitiveness.

However, the idea that wealth floods into Colombia through foreign employment is fallacious, thus far FDI has been typically aimed at resource extraction - wherein mine labourers, banana growers, coffee farmers and similar such workers can expect insulting pay and working conditions; these are issues to which they must resign themselves, for, at around 4% of the workforce, Colombian workers endure the lowest levels of unionisation in Latin America, due in part to the near death sentence entailed by heavy involvement in a trade union, a harrowing tenet of Colombian society hammered home by the 2,500 trade union leaders murdered between 1987 and 1999. Colombians typically receive the butt-end of employment positions by multinational companies, more lucrative jobs in such industries are usually destined to fall into the hands of workers stationed in the corporations' mother country – a group who, unsurprisingly, frequently fall prey to guerrilla kidnappings.

Additionally, whatever remaining public benefits that may arise from the multitudes employed by such companies are frequently undermined by socially destructive policies resulting from the loose rein these companies are permitted. Firstly, due to the relatively minuscule clout Colombia holds in forming trade agreements, such as the Pacific Alliance, foreign organisations can feasibly avoid contributing significant amounts to public coffers.

Another disquieting feature of these firms, in no way limited to multi-national corporations, but something for which they are frequently accused of, is encouraging anti-unionist groups, and trampling on the interests of local, often indigenous, populations. For the former accusation, the ties that over one hundred firms have with paramilitary organisations are alluded to above. As for the latter, ExxonMobil can be singled out for the troubling case study of a mine they have joint-ownership over in the northern Savannah regions, the home of the Wayuu people. The Wayuu people have suffered over 1000 child deaths from thirst and malnutrition over the past year – the cause of this is not the naturally arid area they inhabit, but rather the recent decision to redirect a local river in order to service mining activities. This decision has lead both to repeated crop failures, and the reality of survival on under 1 litre of water per person per day – a community that is now reduced to haranguing the few tourists that pass by for food and money. Egregious practices of this ilk are only possible through the lightening of regulatory oversight conditioned to free trade deals, the endemic corruption that remains in Colombian governance, and the failure to find adequate representation for powerless voices in Colombian society – the aforementioned anti-campesino bias.

As for the latter argument – the need for foreign involvement rather than protectionism for industrial development -whatever merit lies in this claim, it follows still that foreign involvement aids development only if it does not thrive of the social stagnation of its workforce. For example, the breakneck speeds in which Asian nations such as Japan and South Korea have developed, occur as a result of foreign input seeking to better an already well educated workforce through industries such as automotive construction and technology. Additionally, their development was compounded by the protection of domestic firms (i.e. LG, Toyota, etc.), hence allowing the security in their newfound prosperity. As a point of reference, the difference this approach makes is highlighted through juxtaposition with such countries' geographical neighbours, such as Vietnam or the Philippines. In Colombia, the green shoots of a new approach are breaking through, with Colombia quickly becoming a regional hub in the IT and communications industries – a better use for Colombia's well-educated workforce than banana picking or emerald mining.

The consequence of the murky involvement of predatory transnational powers on the peace process is the need for the Colombian government to find a healthy balance between adequate funding for the imperative task of the successful implementation of the conditions for the peace process, with ensuring that it is the Colombian administration that has control over the distribution of funds – so as to serve Colombian interests. One potential positive push in this direction is the promised support of nations such as Norway and Ireland

– who have pledged funding for the developmental facets of the process. Another source is the 9.5 Trillion Colombian Pesos (around $3.2 billion USD) set aside by the Santos administration in order to fund the seismic reforms. However, Senator Roy Barreras suggests that over ten years an estimated $44 billion will be required, for which the gap has been offered to be fulfilled by credit lines from groups such as the IMF, the USA, the EU, and the Word Bank – yet for the reasons outlined above, Colombia should be incredibly cautious of conditions attached to these loans. The Santos administration faces the difficulty of extreme unpopularity, which act as an obstacle to the levying of funds internally – an impasse enhanced by the oligarchic power bloc that Santos represents, which involves an alliance of other powerful families who would react somewhat acerbically if their favourable conditions are threatened, especially when their heavy hands in the electoral machine means that now he needs their support more than ever.

BaCrim bogeymen in the barrios

Threats to the successful implementation of the peace deal are not solely sourced from foreign shores. Quite the opposite, the greatest fears to future flourishing lurk within Colombia's borders – in the burgeoning barrios of Colombia's urban underbelly – and the faceless criminal organisations that haunt them. The threats posed are manifold, the paramilitary successor groups have a considerable stake in the continuation of violence in Colombia, they thrive from a recruitment base of deprived young men, the shred of legitimacy they cling to stems from an ongoing war with guerrillas, a war the belies hidden co-dependency with respect to the different stages of the narcotics supply chain, and their most considerable existential threat is the effectively doubling of military force available to the government towards the end of their eventual destruction. Hence, we can expect paramilitary groups to undermine the peace process wherever possible. Their first affront on this count has been the failed drive of certain groups to attain belligerent status in order to influence the contents of the deal.

Following the final signing of the deal by the guerrillas on August 25th 2016, and the probable ratification the deal will receive at the October 2nd plebiscite, the Colombian authorities have much more yet to fear from the BaCrim threat. The first front where problems present themselves is the handover of municipalities and regions previously governed entirely, or in parallel with, the FARC. Sentiments of self-preservation amongst former FARC fighters, along with frequent low-level interactions between the FARC and the BaCrim paramilitary successor groups, may result in the handover of governance not falling to the state, but to the paramilitary groups. This is because FARC guerrillas previously controlling local governments may feel vulnerable if adequate protection is not provided following demobilisation, hence they may be incentivised to follow the path of certain FARC units, who have defied government and

UN agreements and moved to the demobilisation concentration camps well ahead of schedule. The risk of this occurring was heightened on August 28th 2016, when the FARC agreed to a total, rather than a mere bilateral, ceasefire; hence the firepower no longer exists to support local groups fearing an incursion from paramilitary successor groups before the government arrive to take local control. Shortly afterwards, movements by paramilitary successor groups and the ELN in FARC-controlled areas intensified.

Moreover, this threat does not solely reside in the early retreat of the FARC; it will also take root if the government fails to come good on promises of providing adequate resources for protected governance, or if the promised resources permeate through porous local government purses and into the pockets of corrupt officials. The consequence of, say, an underfunded defence network in a newly governed region, is the constant fear that armed non-state actors seeking to flex their muscles by launching feelers into the vacuum of power left by the removal of guerrillas from the balance of force – can do so in what are likely to be pockets of weakness. This form of conquest ultimately leaves in its wake a costly human toll, and the potential for a brutal local regime intent not on fulfilling an ideological goal, but rather to enrich themselves. Incursions by new groups into handover regions is not entirely confined to paramilitary threats – on a *municipo* by *municipo* basis, FARC governors may join with the FARC fifth front in refusing to heed the conditions of the peace deal, a concern that is especially pertinent in areas of intense coca production, where local FARC operatives sometimes have the appearance more of a localised mafia than a social-democratic movement. Moreover, judging by some of the proclamations from amongst the incoherent garble being emitted by the ELN, there is some reason to believe that ELN forces will seek to expand into former FARC territory before the government can gain a decent footing.

This latter threat is exacerbated by the potential of a sizeable transfer of demobilised FARC guerrillas over to either the ELN, or, surprisingly, the paramilitary successor groups. Whilst some crossover will be inevitable by fighters for whom the battle is ideological, or if, for them, the adventurous guerrilla lifestyle will always be preferable to reintegration into a society hostile to their continued existence – the crossover will be more intense if government provisions for successful reintegration and protection are so lacking that significant numbers of guerrillas believe they will be safer or more fulfilled by retaining their arms and continuing a life on the edges of society.

It is impossible to ascertain any concrete reflection of the probability of the above concern, however, the nature of the threat posed is clear. Whereas at present, due to the conflict being put effectively on hold by the peace negotiations, the tentative balance of power is currently held between the three major power blocs – the Bogotá government, the guerrillas, and the paramilitary successor groups. If the FARC, who comprise the vast majority of remaining guerrillas, succeed in disappearing from the role of a violent actor in the conflict – then the space opened up will fall either mostly to the government, or to the paramilitary groups. If the former happens, then we can hope that Colombia can begin to usher in an epoch of relative peace and stable governance – where discourse does not orbit entirely around the conflict question.

However, if the latter takes hold, we can fear what Gustavo Duncan Cruz has labelled as a *Mexicanisation* of the conflict – where the private armies of cartel leaders brutally slug out their differences both between one another, and with the government. Given the Mafioso nature of this style of conflict, there is little interest for the armed actors to consider themselves to be political agents with the responsibility of acquiring popular support in areas they govern – rather their sole interest is to operate freely outside of the law. Hence in Mexico one can now witness the most profane of human rights offences, coupled with a disquieting degree of governmental coercion. If Colombia is to avoid treading the Mexican post-peace path, then – as is stressed by Carolina Villadiego – successful implementation of the process is key.

How then to beat the bandits? The various armed groups that prowl the Colombian social hinterlands reflect both the first steps, and the dying kicks, of a decades old conflict. Jorge Giraldo Ramírez points to the miraculous turnaround of Medellín to demonstrate a successful model of expelling the grip of criminal organisations.

For intermittent patches of the past few decades, Medellín has held the undesirable accolade of being the most dangerous city in the world, as the battleground for Pablo Escobar's war with the government in the 1990s, and the scene of gang wars between groups vying to take control of the beheaded Medellín cartel after 1993, Medellín has frequently been a microcosm for Colombian violence, with murder rates reaching a peak of 179.78 per 100,000 in 2002 (the Colombian average at the time was 67.0, down from its world leading peak of 79.0 in 1991). Yet the past five years alone have seen Medellín dropped from most international rankings based on crime, to the extent where, provided the dangerous barrios of the North and West are avoided, walking around the city at any time of the day does not leave one racked with a nagging sense of insecurity that hangs over many other Colombian cities.

How has Medellín achieved this? According to Ramírez, through successful central state intervention – which firstly involved the removal of any para-police forces and other non-state groups chipping into the state's supposed monopoly of the legitimate use of force. This was combined with forceful interventions to tackle the leadership, and hence tenability, of the various gangs operating in Medellín. Whilst the task of making the entire city secure has a long way to go, the powerful enforcement of law has been an effective stick in creating large secure areas within the city.

The alternative impositions by the central government have been drives to alter the social conditions that have iteratively spurred people to violence. This has been achieved in part by improvements in provisions for education and public infrastructure (Medellín has Colombia's first metro system), but also the dividend achieved from prosperity within the secure central regions: Medellín can boast a number of thriving, modern universities, such as the Universidad de Antioquia and EAFIT; restaurants, cafés and bars are abuzz with residents and tourists enjoying the social dividend of peace in a beautiful city; industry, including small innovative businesses thriving without fear of civil strife; and a flourishing arts district centred around the barrio Ciudad del Rio. The ends of criminal gangs and successor groups are broadly focused on shortcutting the route to financial gain – hence they lack the ideological rigidity that sustains the previously recalcitrant guerrillas. This means that, by effectively starving their support base through the ample provision of opportunities for young people, and the quashing of those who continue to fight, the last chapter in the unwelcome conflict may finally come to a close.

As the finishing touches, reports are already trickling in suggesting a crime wave in Colombia's ungoverned regions. Particularly in response to an ongoing crackdown on illegal mining operations near the Ecuadorian border, a village leader and three members of the Awa indigenous group have been executed in apparent retribution for speaking out against the mining activities. In this instance, the authorities claim that the mines are operated by the ELN, yet local intelligence points to the *Los Rastrojos* paramilitary's involvement, who operate the nearby mines, especially as the perpetrators were not in ELN uniform. It would appear that fears surrounding the incursion of non-state armed actors in the vacuum left by the FARC has begun to take root, and that the Colombian government must operate with haste for risk of arriving too late into these areas.

Oligarchic hangovers

The handover from colonial rule did not arise from a powerful plebeian revolution, as was the case in, say, the US or Haitian independence movements. Instead, it was a case of a landed oligarchy wrestling control away from their ailing European rulers. As with many Latin American nations, Colombia never experienced any true levelling movement to squeeze the top and bottom wealth brackets closer together. Quite the opposite, the poorest in Colombian society have lived in conditions scarcely improved from feudal colonial rule – in poverty that can rival even the most desperate regions of the Sahel, Sub-Saharan Africa, or South-East Asia – it is even not unusual for villages to lose swathes of their youthful population to malnutrition. In contrast, the elite are split between two predominant groups: rural landowners owning expansive ranches and, in all but legal bond, the campesinos that work their land; and the city elite, sheltered in high-fenced guard-patrolled compounds. Both of whom can continue to protect and build upon their established interests through a clientelist governmental system that functions more on familial connections than genuine meritocracy.

At the top level, one need only scroll through lists of former presidents and cabinet members to see the cyclical repetition of potent surnames and hence gauge the grip they have had over Colombian politics right back to the dawn of the Republic. In a pioneering investigation of the intricate family links between elite Colombians, a Colombian NGO includes on their website a spider's web graph of powerful blood connections within governance, yet investigation beyond this is sparse. A frequently underestimated factor sustaining inequality in Colombia is the high price of university fees – a former adjustment condition for the Colombian economy – as university attendance is the only secure way to avoid national service, only those who can afford the high upfront fees of university attendance (student finance does not exist in the same capacity as the UK in Colombia) can both be educated, and avoid being trained in the art of mortal combat. The middle class, whilst growing, remains nascent, and due to threats to their security, pitiful opportunities, and frequent judicial injustice, it remains too stunted to be an effective force in Colombian discourse – a fact that will hopefully change as a consequence of the peace process.

The aforementioned social divide is reflected in Colombia's persistent occupation of the number eight spot for global inequality, alongside the un-welcome company of Honduras, Central African Republic, and Guatemala. Nowhere is the wealth divide more clear than in rural Colombia, where 64% of the 'best land' is controlled by a mere 0.4% of the Colombian population. Violent land expul-sions and questionable government policies have only accelerated the concentration of land of the past 50 years. Disquietingly, much of the land ap-propriation that has occurred over recent decades has been opportunistic in the haze of violence. No-tably, multinational corporations have not been above organising land invasions, with Oxfam sug-gesting that as many as 40% of Colombians live under some form of contract with multinational corporations. The injustice of inequality has not been lost on Colombians, with over 70% believing that more should be done to the end of redistribution. However, such changes will only be possible when the security situation alters such to allow to freedom for individuals to meaningfully questions the state of affairs.

The political consequence of this degree of inequality is the capture of politics by the oligarchy, resulting in what W. John Green categorised as an 'oligarchic democracy' – a society where elections are guided to provide a pre-ordained result, and ideologies are mere badges for a self-serving and scarcely distinguishable political class. Practices for sustaining the status quo vary in their degree of audacity. Unsurprising practices, such as the ownership of major newspapers by political oligarchs, as is the case with the family of President Santos owning *El Tiempo*, continue to abound in Colombian society, yet are losing their potency due to low-cost news dissemination via the internet. More alarming are practices of electoral fraud, mentioned before, that have remained unchecked throughout Colombian history, including tragicomic episodes where hundreds of deceased voters in certain regions are counted as voting in line with the local *cacique* (some of whom return from the other side to vote more than once in the same election, as

Green notes, "party loyalties run deep in Colombia").

Aside from the visceral sense of injustice this system stirs, it is also a significant barrier to peace. This is because in order to succeed within this milieu, leaders have to balance, and at times play off, the interests of the powerful families that control both public opinion, and, at times, the electoral outcome. Consequently, what changes (or converse lack of) that are made are frequently in the specific interest of Colombian power brokers, hence creating a system that remains necessarily recalcitrant to emancipatory change. We likely will not witness the disappearance of undesirable inequality figures in the immediate future – but, provided the oligarchic colonial hangover does not preclude a successful peace process, a successful peace process will loosen the grip of the oligarchy. This is because the most downtrodden elements of society should be able to enjoy adequate representation and potential unionisation; additionally, a rising middle class can begin to challenge political privileges in society, and hence carve out a chunk of the oligarchy's power, the conflict will be no longer be a political tool for dodging questions about pay, social security, and working conditions, and hence these issues should respond to public pressure and rise up the political agenda.

All of this is hypothetical, but a well implemented peace process will at least create the conditions where these changes will be possible. Democratic social movements are, after-all, possible against an oligarchic system without recourse to violent action. Take the example of the Salvador Allende government in Chile, whilst he ultimately did reach a grisly end after falling foul of Pinochet's CIA-supported coup, he managed to be democratically elected on an emancipatory platform against an oligarchic system that not only had fraudulent sway in the electoral process, but near total control over the press. To circumvent the issue there, the Chilean labour movement spread their word and cultivated class consciousness through stretching the bounds of what was politically permissible in art – for example in the politicised poetry, music and theatre of Victor Jara, Pablo Neruda, and Inti-Illimani. Given the vibrancy of Colombia's cultural scene, an artistically-lead social movement would not be impossible – and could also the be the defining feature of a lasting peace.

One final oligarchic qualm remains; Santos' rule terminates with the general election in 2018. With all major positions up for grabs, the horse-trading and campaigning required to succeed in the election will begin in earnest one year before the pens are put to the ballot. This leaves only one year to devote to the task of successful implementation of a peace process that will require decades of careful management, before the need for short-sighted favour-winning popularity drives take hold. If the immediate results of the peace deal are favourable, then this should not pose a considerable issue. However, if areas of doubt, such as the lenient sentences for convicted FARC war-criminals, or their protected political participation which guarantees them two senate seats, prove unpopular – then rallying against the legacy of the unpopular Santos may provide considerable campaign fodder for ambitious politicians. Nowhere else is this threat more embodied than in the likely presidential successor to Santos, his equally serpentine vice-president Germán Vargas Lleras, who thus far has refused to elicit his stance on the peace process. The fear remains that the social situation may change so that he can launch a campaign that will exploit fears around the process, dampen the implementation, and jeopardise the fragile peace.

Future of the FARC

The structure of the FARC requires all recruits to receive an education, albeit one that is more heavy in Marxist historical materialism and forest survival than econometrics and finance, and to be trained in intense working regimes both in camps and in their relations to the local communities. The organisation also permits the opportunity for individuals to train to take on professional roles such as surgeons (who operate in vast hidden jungle hospitals), and engineers. Consequently, the FARC is constructed of around 7,000 highly motivated and well trained young men and women.

However, their well-earned reputation of neglecting human rights for the end of their struggle, and the vitriolic propaganda that has thrived throughout their existence by painting them as mere terrorists, means that the asset this potential workforce could add to Colombian society is stalled by the likely difficulties ordinary Colombians will face in accepting them back into ordinary life, not least accepting them as a legitimate political force. Forgiving the FARC will be a bitter pill to swallow for many, especially due to the relative impunity the special justice framework will permit them. Consequently, the peace process will have to find an effective means of slowly allowing those who want to re-join society to do so safely – and will have to require the tact that came so naturally to the late Nelson Mandela in convincing the public of the worth of the reconciliation process. There is very little love for the FARC in Colombia, which, whilst just, is yet another threat to a meaningful peace.

Due to the secretive nature of many components of the peace deal, what becomes of the FARC post-deal is as yet unknown. What is clear is that the FARC have been promised guaranteed minor legislative representation, protection for those who enter politics through democratic means, and guaranteed work in demobilising tasks such as de-mining their former zones of control. Beyond that lies a great deal of uncertainty, minor soldiers in the FARC confess the fear they have that, unarmed, they will be targets for brutal retributive acts. This fear has significant historical precedent, recall the fate of the UP following the FARC's last bid for non-violent political action. On this matter, the resolution is simple, protection for former FARC fighters will have to be adequate so as to avoid another political genocide, or a mass migration of fighters to other armed groups. The fear of a repeat of a dirty war on La Violencia scales has, as mentioned, lead a number of FARC groups to abandon their posts early – before the UN and the government have a chance to properly hand over control.

In order to have any hope of attaining political success, the FARC will first have to undergo a serious programming of rebranding; so as to shake off their toxic label. This may require, as with the UP, forming alliances with other political parties to create a unified democratic workers' movement. It may be difficult to win moderate leftist parties over to this cause, yet this is both necessary, given the need for a unified alternative movement to challenge the broadly uniform political hegemony, and possible, given the body of probable support the FARC will carry with them in areas where they have been the only governors, or at least the best of a quite deplorable bunch.

As for the future of those who do not seek political ends, journalist Emily Wright suggests the need to find work that does not count as a huge departure from their guerrilla lifestyle. Initially, de-mining can provide a good outlet that does not require a break-up of their social units nor a full-time return to a nine-to-five job in a world that disapproves of them. In the long run, this style of work can translate to such tasks as forestry management, ecotourism, and sustainable farming. With regards to those wishing to enter normal Colombian life, an important step will be the formal recognition of the skills acquired through their time in the FARC. Understandably, the FARC jungle curriculum is not recognised by Colombian employers, yet the knowledge they have gained in their time as guerrillas could be of considerable value to Colombian society, under the guise of highly motivated and skilled workers – hence the need at the very least for provisions to station guerrillas at the correct level of official qualification that their intelligence merits. Moreover, doing so will reduce the factors that make them easy to be differentiated form other Colombian citizens, and hence a target for employment and physical discrimination. Wright speaks even of meeting FARC doctors and dentists who have acquired their knowledge through off-grid jungle education – to leave uncultivated skills such as these would be nothing short of a farce.

Winning the peace

Colombia finds itself at a crossroads – where the path to be followed will have a profound effect on all facets of everyday life. The details of the agreement drawn up in Havana will determine whether Colombia continues down the path of having a weak, corrupt state, pervasive inequality, and poor political representation – or follows a more (or for that matter, even less) prosperous path. For their part, the state does not show considerable interest in profound change, less than 2% of targeted land restitution has been fulfilled, and the promises of the dominant political parties rarely venture into suggestions that genuinely reflect social justice demands – such as their recalcitrance to minimum wage changes. As such, the main change-minded groups in the process are the FARC and civil society. As outlined in chapter two, if the FARC are to have a hope of winning the peace, in much the same manner as was achieved by the Liberal fighters of the early twentieth Century, they will have to convince the public that their reforms have history on their side. Hence their demands should focus on social issues, such as the role of women in society, and economic issues that permit equitable changes, without reflecting the policies that led to both the erection and eventual demolition of the Berlin wall.

If the FARC are to become legitimate, or even popular, political actors, they can vie to vindicate the changes offered to society in the peace process. As for civil society members, they bring to the table an additional perspective of niche representation, cosmopolitan ideals such as the sanctity of human rights, and much needed aid in the gargantuan task of implementation – the latter tenet being embodied in the work of the legal aid group *Dejusticia*. A final point to note is the veritable need for a meaningful peace in order for any peace to be actually 'won', in much the same way that a meaningful peace relies on a set of social transformations that obliterate the necessity of conflict.

Civil society, the rough collection of organisations that cross contours between the spheres of the family, the market, and the state, has an integral role to play in winning the peace. However, civil society has endured a tough ride throughout recent Colombian history. They have been targeted on one flank for documenting the brutality of armed actors in the conflict, and on the other by the government, under Uribe's claims that everyone from victims' groups to international human rights defenders are in league with the guerrillas. This denunciation was viewed by some sectors of society as a green light for the merciless incursion of anti-civil society violence. However, through the inclusion in the peace process of legal firms, human rights monitors, and victims' groups, to name but a few civil society groups involved, their perception has transformed into a more just reflection of their existence – namely a powerful tool in understanding the nature of the conflict, and it how can be resolved.

As an editorial in *The International Journal of Transitional Justice* by Lucy Hovil and Moses Crispus Okello highlights, however, the involvement of civil society in transitional justice is not without potential pitfalls. The problems with an over-reliance on civil society fall roughly into three main categories: Who funds them? Do they really represent society? And do they undermine the legitimacy of the elected government? The latter is especially important with regards to Colombia, for the situation is not post-autocratic, but rather post-conflict; as such, the state in its present form is not going anywhere. The peace process has respected the first issue through the selection of a diverse range of monitoring groups, especially regarding victims' groups, which are typically bottom-up organisations intent on representing the diverse range of victims left in the wake of the conflict. Therefore, whilst there may be a kernel of truth in the mutually beneficial relationship between guerrillas and some civil society actors, the same can be said for most other interested parties in the resolution of the conflict – hence the need for a diverse selection of groups, to counterbalance competing interests.

As for representation, the cosmopolitan nature of many centrally or internationally organised civil society groups mandates that the difference between Occidental values and Colombian autonomy must be respected, unless we are to take the humanistic view that the same set of social truths hold weight in every society. Even values held sacred in societies where the principle unit of freedom is the individual, such as the unquestioned sanctity of human life, must be examined. For here we must remember that, in the milieu from which groups such as the FARC emerged, the value of the individual is subservient to that of the group – the same can be said of the paramilitaries and their sicarios, yet with enrichment taking the place of the group. A balanced approach in this regard will be one that permits Colombian society to go about this in their own way, whilst calling into question potential excesses that would offend even the most vehement of ethical relativists.

The final matter can be resolved by limiting the role of civil society; civil society can act as an advisor and a watchdog to the government – yet should respect that the government has been elected to govern, and thus should not attempt to muscle away their legitimate role, the Colombian state, after all, is precarious enough as it is. As such, a self-reflexive attitude should be adopted by civil society groups, and the international eyes urging the arrival of peace must remember that civil society groups are run by humans – with all the fallibility that entails. Should the peace deal be signed, another fear emerges from the horizon. That of what Ramírez dubs "bad civil society". By this he means the power that groups existing either on the edge, or outside of the law to influence policy. The effects that this can have of both ushering in socially destructive policies, perhaps an ecologically destructive mining project, or the stalling of implementation of peace process reforms, such as a landowners' group resisting restitution of illicitly acquired land.

One must hope that the above fears are overblown, and that the prudence of those involved and monitoring the peace process will keep in check such threats. To win the peace, all parties involved in the negotiation and implementation will have to transform society in a manner that benefits all Colombians – it appears that the most promising avenues for this are the successful implementation of land reform, the reparation of victims, a drive for social justice, and the integration of peripheral members of society.

Conclusion

Mariano Azuela's masterwork, the novel *Los de abajo* (which roughly translates as 'The Underdogs'), details the struggle of an eclectic band of fighters in the 1915 Mexican revolution. The rag-tag group assemble under the leadership of a charismatic caudillo, fighting at first with strong ideals of civil representation and justice at heart. Yet as the war progresses, and the brutal conflict tears them away from their humanity, they slowly forget the clear-minded intentions they followed, and descend into a foggy haze of violence with no idea for why they are fighting. Frequently *Los de abajo* is considered the definitive book of the Mexican civil war, and also for the numerous political conflicts which have arisen throughout the Latin American continent, perhaps none more so than the Colombian conflict. Colombia has seen a state historically uninterested in governing, peasant-guerrilla forces endangering peasants, and so-called self-defence groups acting as the prime perpetrator of offensive attacks. Over half a century of conflict, the reality of war has muddied the purity of ideals.

When Colombians go to the polls on October 2nd, they must remember that a deal with the FARC will not translate to an immediate cessation of violence in society. The necessary structural changes that have been repeated *ad nausium* throughout this book will take decades to implement – if they even are implemented. Moreover, unwise management or political flip-flopping could hurl Colombia back to the dark days of dirty war. However, the hope offered by the peace deal is too lucrative to refuse – a denial of the accord, unlikely though it is, will send the FARC back into the forests, and potentially into the barrios, to perpetuate their struggle, for they have spent four years negotiating this deal, and hence will not be delighted to accept a host of harsher conditions. This deal is the deal, and there has been ample assistance in forging it. Internal armed political struggle is no longer the zeitgeist in Latin America, the hollow stalemate that acts as a perturbing backdrop to João Guimarães Rosa's novel *Grande Sertão: Veredas* (usually translated as 'The Devil to pay in the Backlands') on the Brazilian civil war describes the recent state of Colombia far better than its nation of origin, as such, an end to the conflict will allow Colombia to shake of the tweniteth century hangover of armed insurrection, opening the space for political participation through pluralist pursuits. In many ways, it seems as though the protracted conflict, and its causes, are the only things holding back Colombia from being a beacon of Latin American prosperity, rather than a basket-case study of how not to run a country.

Why should we care about the process? We can leave aside economic arguments regarding the opportunities surrounding peace in Colombia, indeed, as Cruz suggests, Colombia may have already enjoyed its 'peace dividend'. Instead, we can be hopeful that finally the sharp ache of a violence that has cost over 200,000 lives since 1964, and displaced over ten million people, may finally be remedied. Not only does this bear great humanitarian gains, but the world has much to profit from the cultural asset of a prosperous Colombia, the hope being that a growing flow of travellers, traders, and artists between unexplored areas of this fascinating nation will bring forth a greater understanding and awareness of the diverse beauty of Colombia.

The nagging sense of inevitability that haunts both the cyclical violence in Colombia, and the magical realist style it engendered, can be broken. The turmoil can be quelled, and the long-standing social tumours of corruption, lawlessness, and inequality, can be dampened. The fix, however, will not be easy, and it will not be quick. Yet, in homage to Colombia's greatest author, it may be possible to find peace, in a time of cholera.

Bibliography

Angelo, Paul. N.p., 2016. Web. 9 Sept. 2016.

Arnson, Cynthia and Robin Kirk. *State Of War.* New York: Human Rights Watch, 1993. Print.

Bergquist, Charles W. *Coffee And Conflict In Colombia, 1886-1910.* Durham, N.C.: Duke University Press, 1978. Print.

Bergquist, Charles W. *Labor In Latin America.* Stanford, Calif.: Stanford University Press, 1986. Print.

Bergquist, Charles W, Ricardo Peñaranda, and Gonzalo Sánchez G. *Violence In Colombia.* Wilmington, Del.: SR Books, 1992. Print.

Bergquist, Charles W, Ricardo Peñaranda, and Gonzalo Sánchez G. *Violence In Colombia, 1990-*

2000. Wilmington, Del.: SR Books, 2001. Print.

Braun, Herbert. *The Assassination Of Gaitán*. Madison, Wis.: University of Wisconsin Press, 1985. Print. "Colombia News | Colombia Reports". *Colombia News | Colombia Reports*. N.p., 2016. Web. 2 Sept. 2016.

Durán Crane, Helen. "Reconciliation Through The Environment". *Dejusticiablog.com*. N.p., 2016. Web. 9 Sept. 2016.

Giraldo Ramírez, Jorge. *Guerra Civil Posmoderna*. Bogotá: Siglo del Hombre Editores, 2009. Print.

Giraldo Ramírez, Jorge. "Medellín, From Theater Of War To Security Laboratory". *ResearchGate*. N.p., 2015. Web. 9 Sept. 2016.

Green, W. John. *Gaitanismo, Left Liberalism, And Popular Mobilization In Colombia*. Gainesville: University Press of Florida, 2003. Print.

Hovil, L. and M. C. Okello. "Editorial Note". *International Journal of Transitional Justice* 5.3 (2011): 333-344. Web.

Jackson, Janine. "Humanitarian Nightmare For Colombia's Wayuu Fails To Awaken Corporate Media". FAIR. N.p., 2016. Web. 9 Sept. 2016.

Jacobsen, Nils and Cristóbal Aljovín de Losada. *Cultura Política En Los Andes (1750-1950)*. Lima: Fondo Editorial UNMSM, 2007. Print.

Leech, Garry M. *The FARC*. Halifax: Fernwood Pub., 2011. Print.

Roldán, Mary. *Blood And Fire*. Durham: Duke University Press, 2003. Print.

Sánchez G, Gonzalo and Donny Meertens. *Bandits, Peasants, And Politics*. Austin: University of Texas Press, 2001. Print.

Williamson, Edwin. *The Penguin History Of Latin America*. London: Allen Lane, 1992. Print.

"World Report 2015: Colombia". *Human Rights Watch*. N.p., 2015. Web. 9 Sept. 2016.